爱惜食物

Social Emotional and Multicultural Learning | Non-Fiction Series

Copyright © 2022 by Level Learning, INC. and Washington Yu Ying PCS™
Original and Edited Text Copyright © 2022 by Washington Yu Ying PCS™

All rights reserved. No part of this book in whole or part may be reproduced without written permission from the publisher.

Published by Level Learning, INC.

Content Contributors:
Washington Yu Ying PCS™
Level Learning - Ya-Ching Chang

Illustrations by: Josh Taira

Leveling classification based on Level Learning standard. For full description, visit www.levellearning.com

ISBN 978-1-64040-080-1
Simplified Chinese Edition

About Level Learning:
Level Learning provides a literacy focused curriculum specifically designed for K-12 Chinese as a Second Language classrooms. Our program offers 20 levels of specific and detailed objectives, leveled texts and passages, mastery-based online assessment, and analytics to enable data-driven instruction. Level Learning reading curriculum for both literature and informational text emphasize grammar and comprehension skills to help teachers develop confident and independent Chinese language readers. The non-fiction series of books are specifically designed to support our informational text course based on multiple national standards. To learn more about our entire offering, visit www.levellearning.com.

About Washington Yu Ying PCS™:
Washington Yu Ying PCS is a Mandarin English dual language immersion International Baccalaureate (IB) World school. Yu Ying's mission is to inspire and prepare young people to create a better world by challenging them to reach their full potential in a nurturing Chinese/English educational environment. Yu Ying's comprehensive IB, dual immersion curriculum equips students with global competencies for success in the real world. As a leader in immersion education, Yu Ying is determined to advance Chinese language programs and global citizenry education by helping other schools create and strengthen their Chinese programs. For more information, email: products@washingtonyuying.org

你可能每一顿饭都有东西吃。但是,世界上还有很多人在饿肚子。所以我们要爱惜食物。

你知道吗？每年都有大量的食物被浪费。看看下面的例子，想一想，我们在日常生活中应该怎样减少浪费呢？

吃饭的时候,拿一大堆食物,却经常吃不完。剩下的食物就被丢掉了。

买了一大堆蔬菜水果，放了很久也不吃。不新鲜了就丢掉了。

买一份午餐,只挑自己爱吃的部分。不爱吃的就丢掉了。

只要多留心，这些食物就不会被浪费。我们应该怎样减少浪费呢？

拿食物的时候,先想想自己能吃多少。吃不了的就不要再拿了。

不要一次买太多蔬菜和水果。在蔬菜水果新鲜的时候,就赶快吃完。

吃饭的时候,不要挑食。可以的话,把所有的菜都吃完。

只要我们多留心，减少浪费一点也不难。爱惜食物，从每天的每件小事做起。

Glossary

	Pinyin	English Definition
可能	kě néng	probably
每	měi	each, every
饭	fàn	meal, cooked rice
饿	è	hungry
肚子	dù zi	stomach
爱惜	ài xī	to cherish, to treasure
食物	shí wù	food
大量	dà liàng	a lot of
浪费	làng fèi	to waste
例子	lì zi	example
日常生活	rì cháng shēng huó	everyday life
减少	jiǎn shǎo	to reduce
剩	shèng	left behind
丢掉	diū diào	to throw away
买	mǎi	to buy

	Pinyin	English Definition
蔬菜	shū cài	vegetables
水果	shuǐ guǒ	fruites
久	jiǔ	(long) time
新鲜	xīn xiān	fresh
午餐	wǔ cān	lunch
挑	tiāo	to pick out
留心	liú xīn	to pay attention
拿	ná	to take
赶快	gǎn kuài	at once, quickly

www.ingramcontent.com/pod-product-compliance
Lightning Source LLC
Chambersburg PA
CBHW041221070526
44584CB00001B/44